COMPTON WYNYATES

FROM THE MOAT

WILIAM MARQUIS OF NORT

LONDON

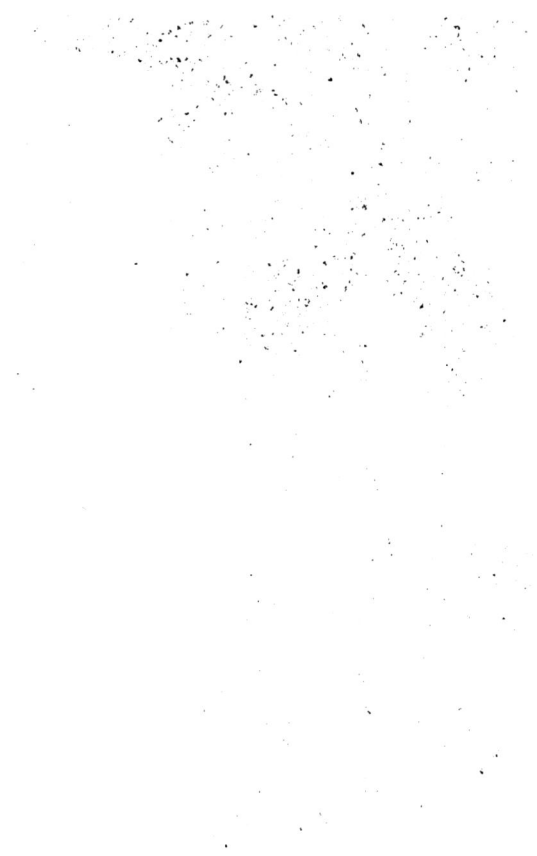

COMPTON
WYNYATES

BY

WILLIAM MARQUIS OF NORTHAMPTON

LONDON

ARTHUR L. HUMPHREYS, 187 PICCADILLY, W

1904

TO HER WHO FOR EIGHTEEN YEARS SHARED
AND LOVED THIS HOME, AND WHO WAS
THE CENTRE OF ITS BEAUTY
AND PEACEFULNESS.

CONTENTS

v

ILLUSTRATIONS

HOUSE FROM THE APPROACH.

COMPTON

CHAPTER I

The old house of the Comp...
... ...
... ...
... ...
known as Compton it ... ...
evidently n t a pet name, nor, a'd
... ... antiquarian, it is to
Philip Co z of Henry VIII, grand-
... ... the ...
of H... ... ...
until ... ...
with ... ...
a way ... ...
I am the ... and ... the ... ... first
view of the house looking ... you ... the ... ...
above, it less it appear to be in a here ... ...

1

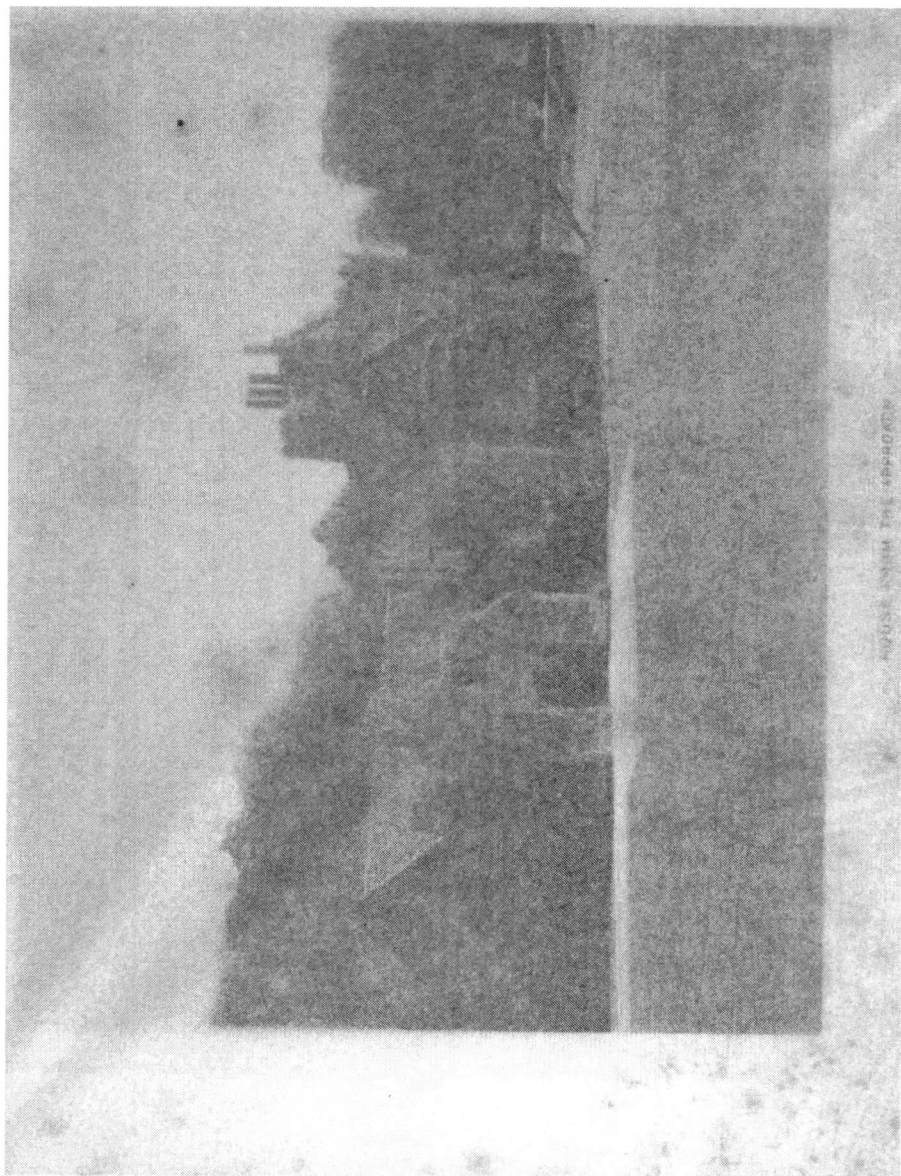

COMPTON WYNYATES.

CHAPTER I.

NAME—POSITION—ORIGIN.

THIS old home of the Compton family seems to *Name* have been called sometimes Compton Wodyates —the gate of the woods; sometimes Compton Wynyates —the gate of the vines and vineyards; and was also known as Compton-in-the-Hole. This latter name was evidently not a nickname, for, although it does not sound very complimentary, it is to be found in the Royal Charter of Henry VIII., granting the use of the Royal Lion on the family arms, and also on an old map of 1610 by John Speede. It is an ungraceful, but not untruthful, allusion to the position of the house; for, while woods and vineyards have disappeared and only a suspicion of vine-covered terraces are to be seen round the combes, it must be confessed that the first view of the house, looking down from the high road above, makes it appear to be in a hole. In old times, before roads existed, the house was so hidden away in the surrounding combes and trees, that a pike, which is still preserved, was erected on the heights above in order to mark the place for visitors and travellers. The name Compton Wynyates is very descriptive. The 'ton' or hamlet in the Warwickshire 'Combe' (*Cwm* in the British and *Cumbe* in the Saxon, meaning valley) gives the family name; and when the sloping combe-sides were terraced, and grapes were grown and turned into what was then called wine, the house must have stood at the entrance or gate of the vineyards. On the London property belonging to the Comptons there is a Wynyatt Street, probably named after the Warwickshire house; but it is an odd coincidence that it is close to the spot where the monks of Clerkenwell used to cultivate their vineyards, on the slopes now occupied by six-storied workmen's dwellings. The reason for the site in Warwickshire is as obvious as the existence of London on the Thames. Water was the first necessity, not only for drinking and for fish-ponds, but also for defensive purposes, as a moat surrounded the house; and there was certainly a second moat, or bit of water, giving a double protection before the only entrance on the south-west could be reached. An old engraving, which the writer once saw, shows the house with large ponds, far exceeding in size anything that exists

2

HOUSE FROM THE "BEST GARDEN"

now; but, as even during the last twenty years the *Position* water supply has diminished, it is possible in old days that, at this particular spot in the combes, water was very abundant, and it was this that tempted the Comptons to fix their home here.

Unfortunately there are no family papers and no old plans. There is nothing to determine the original history of the house, and therefore conjecture has to take the place of fact: and imaginings tempered by reasoning and helped by local knowledge must supply a very slight description of a place, which, if the whole truth were known, should give one of the most interesting histories that an old English home could afford. The house, surrounded and almost hidden on three sides by grassy hills, on which the trees lovingly grow, is a picture which can be best described by the two words 'romantic' and 'restful.' It is difficult to give the first sensations of the visitor when, driving past the small church, the old dovecot, and the queer-shaped blue-box trees, and, turning a corner, the house comes suddenly in sight. It has often been said: 'The first sight took away my breath.' It has been the experience of members of the family who know the place well to give a kind of gasp and almost to cry out. Certainly no one can see it and remain unmoved. One is carried away from this world and into some other where the supernatural would be

8

Origin quite at home, and where anything trivial or modern
or practical would be out of place. No description
could be given in words, and those who have attempted it have failed. But to those who love the
place it has sometimes appeared odd that distinguished writers have been so little able to convey
any idea of its beauty. O. W. Holmes visited it,
and wrote afterwards that he had enjoyed eating
peaches in the garden! Stow got as far as saying
that it is a place not without its pleasures. Howitt
writes of the 'stillness,' the 'dreaminess,' the 'en-
chanted region,' the 'perpetual loneliness;' but to
those who live there the word *rest* conveys the inner-
most feeling. The house seems to rest upon the green
lawns as if it could float away at any moment. It
rests there as a butterfly settles on the flower that
shows off its beauty best. The air is full of the
cawing of rooks, the lowing of cattle, the cooing of
the doves, the barking of a distant dog, and the
chiming of still more distant church bells; but the
house in its setting remains undisturbed, and, though
children may laugh and shout around it, the spirit of
man is quieted by its restfulness.

Nothing is known as to the home of the Compton
family before the accession of Henry VIII. Collins
states that the family is descended from Turchid, son
of Alwyn, contemporary with Edward the Confessor

4

BAY WINDOW IN COURTYARD.

and William the Conqueror. Turchid did not side *Origin.*
with Harold, and was left in possession of his estates,
including the lordship of Compton. His sons and
descendants (Arnulphus, Osbertus, and Waleranus de
Cumton), in the reigns of Henry II., Richard I., and
John, held land under the first Earl of Warwick, to
whom William Rufus had given Turchid's Warwickshire properties. Philip de Cumton figures in the
fifth year of John as joint witness to a grant of land
in Tysoe (a village less than a mile away) made to the
Canons of Kenilworth. Therefore it is not unreason-
able to believe that they lived at Compton Wynyates,
especially as in the seventh year of Edward I. another
Philip de Cumton was Lord of the Manor of Compton
Wynyates, and held it by the service of half a knight's
fees. We also find Robert ('dominus de Cumpton'),
Thomas, Edmund, William, and Robert as patrons of
the church of Compton during the years 1304–1462.

What the house was like in those days we have
no idea, but it seems likely that before it assumed
its present shape in Tudor times there was on this
spot the home of the Compton family. Perhaps it
was an old English timber house, such as was the
fashion before the Tudors, but even the present brick
and stone house is not all of one date or design. A
superficial examination soon proves that all the projecting features that form the picturesque grouping

and sky-line, including the galleried chapel, are additions to the original simpler form of the house; and as the earliest of these was undoubtedly added 1512–1520, it seems certain that in Henry VII.'s reign there was a brick house which forms part of the present building. The west side, where the original eaves and windows are preserved, affords the best idea of the character of the oldest house, as it is easy to omit in the mind's eye the added octangular turrets. The difficulty is great in determining the dates of the various additions and alterations, as some of these may have followed very quickly on the building of the main block itself. There may have been changes during the process of building, or more probably enlargements of the original idea, either for increased comfort and convenience, or for beauty. There is the further difficulty that old materials were available from Fulbrooke Castle, so that it is not possible to deduce facts from differences of material. The bricks, with the exception of the additions of Queen Anne's time, appear to be the same throughout. What wonderful bricks they are! Their colour gives the house one of its great charms, for they vary in different lights. They are so dark and deep-coloured on grey days, so bright and brilliant in the sunshine, and when the setting sun throws its last rays through the trees, the house blushes pink at the

... the ... there ... which ... chapel, are additions ... of ... form of the house; and ... ... wainscot ... lly added 1512 ... ... in Henry VII's reign ... ... forms part of the ... ... west ..., where the original ... ... see ... wainscot, the last ... ... of a ... West house, as it is easy ... ... mind's ... ... old octangular ter- ... ... beauty is ... in determining the dates of the ... ... and alterations, as some of the ... ... very quickly on the building ... ... here may have been ... ... of building, or ... ... the original idea of her f ... ... at ... convenience, or for beauty. There is ... further difficulty that old materials were available ... ... belic sales to the, so that it is not ... ... differences of material. ... ... option on the additions of ... ... to be the same through- ... ... it is they are! their colour ... ... has great charms, for they ... ... they are sober, and deco- our and ... ... so bright and brilliant to the small ... ... as the setting sun throws its last rays through ... ... on the house looks pink at the

6

GARDEN IN WINTER

good-night greeting. Where were the bricks made *Origin* that now cannot be copied? Probably on the spot, for below the house, near the long pond, when laying a drain, workmen came upon the remains of open brick kilns with bits of the same coloured bricks, and also found traces of rows of steps on which the bricks were dried. An experiment has been tried with the clay near at hand, but the colour cannot be reproduced. Is it because we are in too great a hurry with our baking? In the older days with wood fires it was a slow process and the result would be more satisfactory. Alas! the rage for saving time robs the world of much that would be beautiful in Art. To the fumes of the burning wood the peculiar bluish glaze at the end of the bricks is attributed, and with them the diaper pattern on the walls is produced.

Infinite care was taken; much time was spent on the family home. The fancy of a man of taste was gradually carried out, and thus we have irregular but quite harmonious architecture; a lovely colour, every detail in the best style; the whole in a wonderful setting combining to make a picture which all must admire, and which the happy possessor may be pardoned for calling a vision of beauty.

7

CHAPTER II.

ARCHITECTURE.

THE building of the present house, or its enlargement and embellishment, took place, as stated above, before 1520, and here again a distinction must be made, as some parts of the additions are undoubtedly much older. Dugdale states, on the authority of *Leland's Itinerary*, that a great part of the materials of which the house was built came from Fulbrooke, a distance of fourteen miles. John, Duke of Bedford, brother of Henry V., had built there early in the fifteenth century a noble Tower, described by Rous ' as good as a castle, a castle of brick and stone.' Before this Joan, Lady Abergavenny, had built there a fine gatehouse of stone, and also a lodge, in the time of Richard II. The buildings were in ruin in 1478, and when Sir William Compton was appointed Keeper of Fulbrooke Park in the beginning of Henry VIII.'s reign, he had permission to pull them down, and make use of the materials for his new house.* There is a tradition that the lovely twisted

* Collins states that he rebuilt Compton, 'the seat of his ancestors'— but rebuilding may mean beautifying.

8

Open Yard

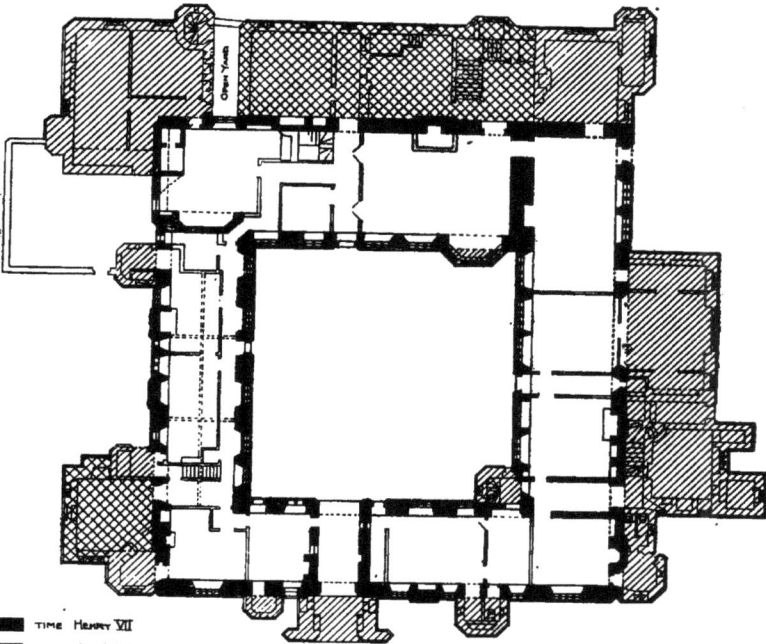

TIME HENRY VII
TIME HENRY VIII
LATER ADDITIONS

GROUND PLAN OF COMPTON WYNYATES

TERMINATIONS OF HOOD MOULD OVER THE BAY WINDOW.

chimneys came from there, but as they are like the *Architecture*
chimneys at Hampton Court, they are probably of
Henry VIII.'s time. It is tolerably certain, however,
that the greater part of the bay-window of the Hall
is of older date, for two reasons—the two carved
heads that form the termination of the hood-mould
over the arched heads of the window openings have
a coiffure and head-dress of earlier times than
Henry VIII., and the Comptons' crest (a demidragon erased gules within a coronet of gold granted
by that king) above the centre window is a separate
piece of stone, which would hardly have been the
case unless it were an addition. Another similar
crest inside is also an addition, and in this case the
lower half of the shield is detached from the stone-
work behind. The traceried band in which the
shields occur has obviously belonged to a different
and smaller bay window, because the wider panel
which contains the shields is no longer in the centre,
having three panels on the right and four on the
left. The stone jointing shows that the centre panel
on the left is an addition required for the greater
width of the bay in which it is now placed. The
battlemented parapet over this band is a further
addition, possibly added when the eaves were removed
and the walls heightened. The upper part of the
bay, therefore, is of a composite structure, partly

9

c

Architecture of Henry VIII.'s time and partly later, while the whole of the lower part is of older date, and probably was brought from Fulbrooke.

The ceiling of the great hall was also brought from another house. The wooden principals of the roof do not fit in with the windows; the carving is of older date than the house, and is a patchwork. The louvre was probably filled up at this time. But of this any certainty is impossible, because the chimney and certainly the existing mantel are of later date, as the window above the mantel—which, when open, would hardly have allowed space for the chimney—was filled up in Queen Anne's time. The screen, with its quaint carvings and linen-pattern panels, appears to be of earlier date than Henry VIII., and may also have been brought with the ceiling from Fulbrooke. Here again is a difficulty, as in the centre is a panel giving a curious representation of a battle* or tournament combined with the arms of Compton, with the augmentation of the lion of England and chevron, granted by Henry VIII. It appears, however, that this panel is an insertion, for if the back be examined, although it is linen-folded as the other panels, the work is much smoother and less vigorous, and may therefore be an imitation of

* Perhaps the Battle of Tournai in France, where Sir W. Compton was knighted.

10

CHANCELS

also b...
...nipals...
...earl...
...pearl-work...
...costume...
...l...
...ntal are...
...mented wit...
...space for...
...there...
...line pattern...
...Henry VII...
...with the c...
...difficulty,...
the cornice is...s represen...
...ted with the...
...on of the h...y of
...Henry VII. ...
...an insertion f...
...it is lamentable...
...smoother a...
...an imitation...

...Sir W. C...

THE HALL

the older ones. Again, it may be noticed that in *Architecture*
some of the windows the spandrels are partly filled
with carving, partly hollow. It is possible that the
more ornamented may have been brought from
Fulbrooke. In considering this, the two windows
opening into the court from the dining-room and
ante-chapel should be examined. The dining-room
originally extended much further. The wooden
cornice goes the whole length of that side of the
house. When the chapel was added by Sir W.
Compton, the partition was built between the dining-
room and ante-chapel, and as the light from the
larger window was cut off, the present window
in the dining-room was inserted. The difference
between the two windows is apparent, and, as
suggested above, they may be of different dates, or
one or both may have been brought from Fulbrooke
and added to. The cutting of the wooden cornice,
where the large entrance was made out of the
original wall into the chapel, is very primitive.

From all these indications it seems certain that
Sir William Compton beautified by additions and
adornments a plain square house, which can be
traced by the yard-thick outer wall, the plinth of
which can be still seen on the kitchen wall inside
the N.W. corner, and also in the chapel. The west
side shows what the plainer house must have been

Architecture like, with wooden window frames. The four stone roofs mark the four sides. Two of these roofs end in noggin gables on the south side, which have carving under the projecting windows. The addition of the N.W. corner is very apparent, as it bisects the older gable, and while one iron clamp to strengthen that gable is outside the addition, the other is inside one of the bedrooms. The old oak ceiling, which is visible on the bedroom floor from the centre of the south side and extends along the whole north side and to the end of the Minstrels' Gallery, is uniform. It is likely that this ceiling continued over the front hall before it was removed to make way for the present higher ceiling brought from elsewhere. The extra piece of wall at the east end of the hall may have supported the older ceiling. There does not seem to be any other explanation for it.

It is just possible that Sir William Compton built a plain square house, and subsequently, as he grew richer from all the properties given him by his friend, Henry VIII., he embellished it; but as his father and grandfather were in such a position in the time of Henry VII. that on the death of his father he became the ward of the King and the playmate of the King's second son, it is more likely that the plainer square brick house is of the time of Henry VII., and all the improvements, includ-

'THE BARRACKS,' WITH SLOPING ROOF BEAMS.

.

ing the carved porch, were made in the time of *Architecture*
Henry VIII. The traditional date is 1520; and as
Sir W. Compton was fighting in France in 1513, and
received a royal licence to empark additional land
in 1519, the actual date is between 1515 and 1520.*
Since that date certain alterations in the structure
have taken place.

1. The Barracks, so called because soldiers are
supposed to have used this part for a dormitory,
hacking niches out of the floor beams for their
sleepy heads, have at some period been arranged
along the whole length of the eastern side under
the roof, and at the same time an addition may
have been made to the highest part on the S.E.
The saddle-back roof on the tower is certainly an
addition, the roof-timbers there being an adaptation
of materials made for some other portion, and the
outer staircase-turret is roughly attached to older
chimneys. At a later period these barracks were
turned into a row of rooms, as has been the case
on the south and west side, where the partitions
bisect the oak-beamed ceilings. It appears that
originally there were long open rooms, some for
visitors sleeping in rows, and some for the servants
and retainers. Privacy does not seem to have
existed in the good old Tudor days, and washing

* Plan, showing old square house, with additions of 1515 and 1732.

13

chitecture as it is practised now would have been considered unnecessary, unhealthy, and a temptation of Providence.

Many of the oak ceilings in the rooms were hidden by lath and plaster, and there may be more still to be discovered. When one of the plaster ceilings was lately taken down in a lower room, coins of Charles II. and James II. fell out. They must have dropped through the chinks of the floor above, out of the pocket of some gay Cavalier.

2. In the reign of Queen Anne (or perhaps by James, fifth Earl of Northampton, about 1732) a wing was built at the back of the great hall, over what must have been an open terrace. Two windows were blocked up, but can still be seen. Under the new wing is a crypt with the Roman cross vaulting in brick on square pillars, as used at that period. In this crypt or cellar the rough stone under wall can be seen. It is probable that all the foundation work of the house is constructed of similar rough rubble, made of the local stone. The foundations may be of much earlier date than the brick house, stone being the common material of the locality; bricks being the novelty and luxury. This Queen Anne's wing had sash windows of wood, and was panelled inside and finished in the style of the period. In 1860 alterations were made by Sir Digby Wyatt to bring it more

14

...as ...   ...e been...
...   a templat...

                            ...n the ro... ...were ll...
                            ...e may be more so...
                            ...of the plast...
                            ...wer rooms...
                            ...t. They ...t have...
                            ...of the ... ...ove. On
                   Cave...
   ...   ...s... ... for...
   ...   ...e..n, about l...
   ...   f the g eat l...
   ...   ...a terrace. Two ...
   ...   ...s stil be seen. T... ...the
...   ...th the Roman cro s vaulting
in...   ...ors, as us I a... ... ...l... in
t...   ...ec... .he road... ...under wall can
...   is...   ...t... ...ne fou... ...ou work
   ...   ...ilar rough rubble.
   ...   ...r al...s may be of
   ...   k leec... ...ne ising the
   ...   ...ality...l is being the
   ...   Qu en...s... wing had
   ...   ...nd we... ... inside and
   ...   the p... ...i...3 altera-
... is...   Plate... ...der it more
                            51

into harmony with the older house. It was also in 1860 that the principal staircase with a bay window took the place of a smaller staircase; and an entrance into the drawing-room from the stairs was effected by means of a corner gallery with great stone brackets and a large open hood or canopy. This was all removed and a small balcony in harmony with the other woodwork in the hall was substituted in 1890.

3. It may have been the same James, Earl of Northampton, who, to heighten the walls of the court-yard in order to get rid of the drip, removed the eaves, the difference of the bricks being easily discernible. It was at all events in 1732, for they bear that date, that the water-pipes were added, with large characteristic heads. Those in the court were rendered necessary by the alteration of the roofs. At one time the windows towards the court in the drawing-room and below it in the dining-room were blocked up, possibly to make the rooms warmer, or to avoid the window tax.

It was about 1732 that sash windows were put in the east front as far as the chapel. These appear in engravings in the beginning of the nineteenth century, and were removed and replaced by Gothic windows in 1860, at the same time that a bay window was thrown out of the drawing-room and a new door made.

Architecture At the south-western corner an addition was made, probably at the same time (1732), and a stone outside chimney was added later.

This completes the tale of the present building; and to sum up, it may be stated that an older house was succeeded by a plain square brick house in the reign of Henry VII. Large additions were made about 1515–1520, further additions and alterations in 1734, and a few alterations in 1860. But these two latter changes have not much interfered with the general character of the house, which is one of the best specimens of unspoilt Tudor work in England.

SOUTH WEST VIEW OF THE HOUSE.

CHAPTER III.

IN 1768 occurred the dismantling of the house, *The House after 1768* which in 1859, and even later, was looked upon by the county people as an uninhabitable ruin. The reason of the dismantling and closing of the house was a contested election! The borough of Northampton at that time was divided in its allegiance between three county nobles, Lord Spencer, Lord Halifax, and Lord Northampton. It is doubtful that any politics entered into the question, but a family rivalry seems to have existed. An election took place in 1768, of which accounts are preserved. While the election lasted, for all who were thirsty, beer ran in Althorp Park, at all the cross-roads, and probably also at Castle Ashby and Horton. Other liquors were supplied, as it is stated that the electors, having drained Lord Halifax's cellars of port, were given claret. This was not strong enough, so they migrated in a body to Castle Ashby and its port. The election over, next came the scrutiny, not as afterwards by half-a-dozen members of the House of Commons, but by the whole House, and each of the peers enter-

17   D

tained members to obtain their support. Forty covers were laid daily at Spencer House, and as many at the houses of the two other noblemen. It was at length decided in favour of Lord Spencer, who then had to nominate the member, the votes having apparently been given for the peers, and not for candidates. He had so much difficulty in finding one, that eventually, so runs the story, he nominated a man who was in the East Indies. All this seems ludicrous, but it was a serious matter to the families concerned. The expenses were enormous. Lord Spencer was said to have spent nearly 130,000*l*., and the debt was only paid off after many years.

Lord Halifax was ruined, and his estate, with its unfinished house, sold. Lord Northampton, besides cutting down all his old timber to the amount of 50,000*l*., sold most of his furniture from Castle Ashby, and the whole of that from Compton Wynyates, and spent the rest of his life in Switzerland. Before going abroad he gave orders that the Warwickshire house should be pulled down, as he could not afford to keep it up. This, however, Mr. Birrell (the agent) deferred doing on various excuses, patching up bad roofs, &c., as well as he could afford. The family owes him an eternal debt, for he not only saved the house, but planted many of the present trees. One result of the closing of the house has been that since

18

1768, members of the family have been buried at *The House after 1768* Castle Ashby, instead of in the family vault under the church near the older home. From this time a corner of the house was furnished and used by the tenant of the home farm or agent until 1880, when a separate house was built for him, and new stables were erected. The stables which were then removed were at right angles in front of the S.W. corner of the house, and dated probably from James, Earl of Northampton, in the beginning of the eighteenth century. Only a stone doorway and a sundial remain. There were also other buildings to the south of the house which have all disappeared. As regards the grounds, the plantation and yew hedge were planted about 1877 and 1880, and in 1895 an enclosed field to the east was turned into a garden. After this was made, an old labourer said that that plot of ground had always been called 'the best garden.' The old name has been restored, and the luxuriance of the flowers seems to give the idea that they have only been sleeping for over 150 years, and are glad to be called again into life and beauty.

Above the best garden may be seen, between two elms, a hollowed bit of ground, which may have been a skittle alley or bowling green. The ground above has always been known as the bowling-alley field. Perhaps it was here that Sir William Dugdale played

The House after 1768 skittles with Sir William Compton, second son of Spencer, Earl of Northampton, killed at Hopton Heath, for in the fly-leaf of a diary kept by the former in 1644 there is a pencil note in abbreviated form: ' 22nd June laid out in skittle garden silver and pencils for Sir William Compton, 2/8.' It must be added, in justice to the memory of Sir William, that a line has been drawn through the words, and it may therefore be presumed that the debt was honourably paid. A Dugdale brought the diary to Compton Wynyates a few years ago, and another William Compton discovered the entry!

Some details must now be given as to the house itself. The gateway is highly ornamented, and from it the drawbridge over the moat, which was filled up in the time of Cromwell, was drawn up and let down. The wearing of the stone shows where the chains went. Over the entrance appear the arms of England with a dragon and greyhound as supporters (*temp.* Henry VII. and Henry VIII.). The arms are surmounted by a Royal crown, on which is inscribed DOM REX HENRICUS OCTAV. Below, among the carvings, can be seen the rose of England and pomegranate of Granada interlaced, an unintentional satire on the union of Henry and the unfortunate Queen Catherine. On each side are the Tudor roses with crowns. In the spandrels are : on one side the Portcullis, badge of

20

WINDOW IN HENRY VIII'S ROOM

COMPTON WYNYATES

Henry VIII., and on the other a badge of Catherine of Aragon, composed of the castle of Castile, the pomegranate, and the sheaf of arrows, the badge of her mother, Isabella. This latter can also be seen on the tomb of Prince Arthur at Worcester. It will be noticed that at the lowest ends of the curved label mould are two little figures, a man and woman dressed in the fashion of a much later period. These have been stuck in at a subsequent date, probably by James about 1730. There is a beautiful iron Gothic guichet taken from the front door and now hanging in the hall, through which the porter could look at those who approached the house. It has been removed to prevent its being more broken, or stolen. There were also small windows, and a small staircase on each side of the gate, which all show how carefully the porter had to guard the safety of the house in times of war and trouble. The small window to the left was open, and a tray was placed outside it with food for the poor who called. Opposite, on the stones, can be seen the marks where arrows were sharpened. The drawing-room was panelled in 1859. The ceiling is original and of the time of Elizabeth. Nash, writing about the time of the restoration of the house, in 1859, says : 'The ceiling of this apartment and that of the room called Henry VIII.'s chamber are the original ceilings judiciously restored.' The chimney-piece (with

21

ugly additions by Sir D. Wyatt) and the panels came from Canonbury Tower in Islington, the gate-house of the country seat of Sir John Spencer, whose only daughter eloped with Lord Compton in the reign of Elizabeth. This story will be told in the chapter on the family.

The only stained glass is in the room called Henry VIII.'s room, consisting of four pieces, giving the arms of England and Aragon; and two other small pieces above the door near the chapel—the dragon crest of the Comptons.

The chapel once contained a stained-glass window: the Crucifixion above, and below Sir William Compton and two sons kneeling on the left, and his wife and two daughters kneeling on the right. A dedicatory window was presented to Balliol College Chapel by Sir William Compton, but no trace of either can now be found.* There are four curious pieces of wood

---

* Dugdale says : ' In the chapel within this house was a costly window of rare workmanship, the Passion of our Saviour being therein very lively represented ; and in the lower part thereof his own portraiture, as also that of his lady, both kneeling in their surcoats of arms.' Further, after regretting the destruction of the tombs in the church, he says : ' So that in place of them (whereof I was not so happy as to take notice while they stood), I shall here to the memory of that worthy person, who was the first rayser of this house . . . . Sir W. Compton, and to the honour of the family, insert the portraiture of him, his lady, and children, as they still remain (having been set up in his time) in the chapel of Balliol College in Oxford.' The inscription is : ' Wilhelmus Compton Miles, cum pia consorte sua hanc fenestram vitrari fecit A⁰ DNI—1530.'

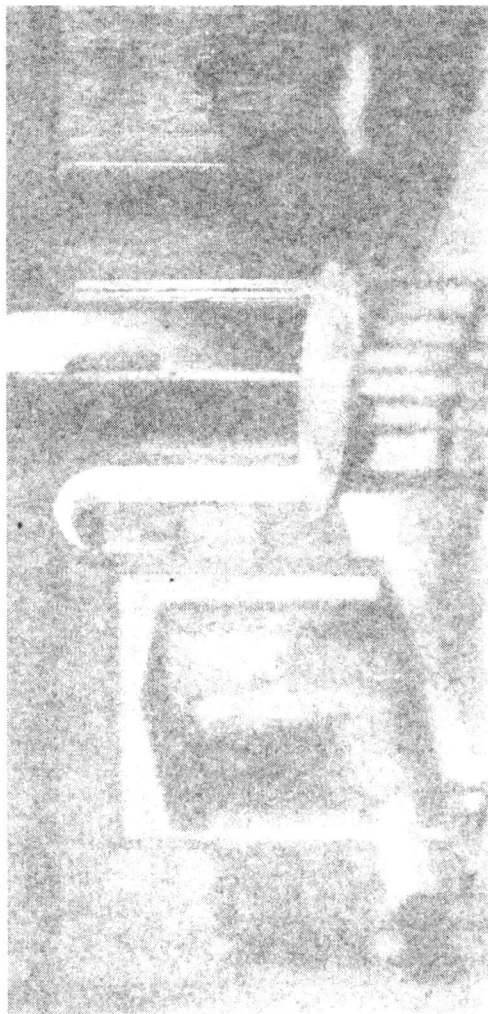

GUARD ROOM.

carving over the screen in the chapel. On one side the Coronation of the Virgin and the buffeting, the carrying of the Cross, and the Crucifixion of Christ; on the other side the seven deadly sins are portrayed by individuals, who, committing the sins, are being conveyed by devils to Satan on the backs of infernal beasts; and another panel probably represents the nine wise men. The galleries of the chapel have been lately restored.

The highest part of the house contains a room called the guardroom, with secret rooms and an oubliette; and above is a room called the Priest's room, owing to the wooden slab in the window being marked with five crosses. Here there is a cinque-cento Italian door, which may have been carved by an Italian priest, who was kept in hiding and who thus employed his leisure time, and also in painting fruits and flowers round the small window over one of the staircases. The numerous means of exit from this room are curious, and indicate the dangers of the time.

Out of what is now called the Cavalier's room is a little room, and above this another which was only found by the accident of a child tumbling against the wall, which gave a hollow sound and led to the finding of the door, then whitewashed over like the walls.

The wearing of the brick stairs is very remarkable,

as only a very large amount of use can have thus worn them away. There are several legends as regards this room. One is that a skeleton was found in it with its bony feet in a pair of leathern slippers. Another is that an overturned table and a gauntlet were found, but unfortunately the articles named cannot be produced. It will be remarked that all over the house there are numerous niches in the walls. The use of them is unknown, but the most probable theory is that lights were placed in them before candles and oil-lamps were in use.

24

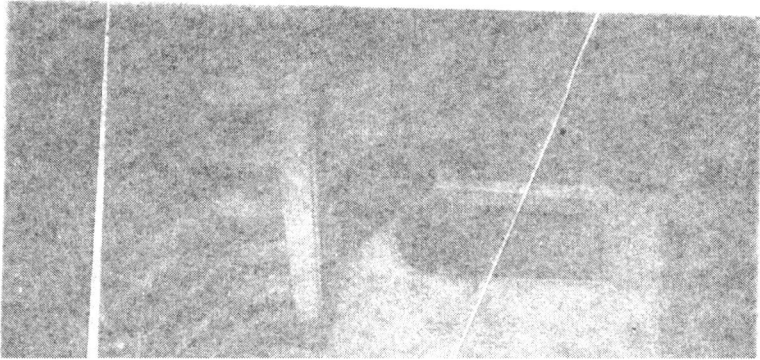

... of ash can ...
... several legends as ...
... skeleton was found i...
... of leathern slippers.
... ed.
...
... in...
... known, but ...
were placed in ...
were in use.

PRIEST'S ROOM

CHAPTER IV.

HISTORY OF THE COMPTON FAMILY TO THE CIVIL WAR TIME.

HAVING given this short history of the house, a reference to those who have lived in it, and its various vicissitudes, may be of interest. Mention has already been made of the Comptons in the first reigns after the Conquest. The first knight of the family is Sir Robert Compton, knighted before 1303 by Edward I. His son Robert was a soldier and a knight for Warwickshire in the Parliament held in 6 Edward III. The allowance for his and his colleagues' expenses for an attendance of ten days was 6*l.*; but in the following year, for twelve days' attendance, they only received 4*l.* 16*s.* Robert's son and grandson were coroners for Warwickshire ('an office of very great account'), and the latter's widow presented her second son to the Church of Compton. Their great-grandson Edmund died in the eighth year of Henry VII., and was succeeded by Sir William Compton, who erected the house as it now is, and who, by his prominent position at the Royal Court, may be said to have started the fortunes of the Compton family.

He was left a minor, eleven years of age, at his father's death, and, being a ward of the Crown, was appointed to attend on Henry, Duke of York, the King's second son. Being thus brought up with the future Henry VIII., he became such a favourite that, on Henry's accession to the throne, he was appointed Groom of the Bedchamber. Fuller tells us that 'no layman in the Court except Charles Brandon, in whom affection and affinity met,' was nearer to the King than he. He received many proofs of the King's affection, for he possessed large landed estates in twenty-one different counties, among them that of Ashby Davids (or Castle Ashby) in Northants, the family's chief home at the present time. He was also presented with 'a mansion called Lovell's Inn, situate in Paternoster Row, within the city of London.' Collins quotes curious stories of the increasing friendship between the King and his favourite :—

'On January 12.15.10. The King being informed that divers gentlemen had prepared themselves to just, he elected Mr. Compton for his companion; and being suitably armed in the little park of Richmond, came to the justs unknown to all persons and unlooked for, and performed so gallantly, that the two strangers had great praise; but at length in a

26

WYNYATES

... d the fortunes of the

... teen years of age, at his
... ward of the Crown was
... years old of York, the King's
... he up with the future
... favourite that, on
... he was appointed
... tells us that the
... Charles Brandon, in
... was nearer to the
... profits of the King's
... landed estates in
... ing them that of
... by, in Northants, the
... present time. He was also
... called Lovell's Inn, situate
... the city of London,
... increasing friend-
...

... being informed
... themselves to
... panion; and
... of Richmond,
... persons and
... probably, that the
... at length in a

GATEWAY

course, by misfortune, Sir Edward Minto, brother to *The Family*
the Lord Abergavenny, running against Mr. Compton, *History to*
hurt him sore, and he was likely to die. This en- *the Civil War*
deared him more to the King.'

'On November 2nd the same year, at his court
of Richmond, His Majesty caused proclamation to
be made that he with his two aids, Charles Brandon
and Mr. Compton, would answer all comers with the
spear at the tilt one day, and at turney with swords
the other; and accordingly on Nov: 13, they entered
the field richly apparelled, their bases and trapper
being cloth of gold set with red roses, ingreiled and
embroidered with gold; and, having valiantly performed before divers strangers of the Emperor Maxi-
milian's court, the ambassador of Spain, &c., had the
prize adjudged to them.'

In 1510 he was appointed Constable of Sudley
Castle, Master of the Hunt and Park-keeper; in
1513, Usher of the Black Rod before the King or
his Lieutenant at the feast of St. George in Windsor
Castle, with a fee of twelve pence per diem. The
same year he went with the King to Calais in
command of 400 men. He commanded the rear-
guard; 800 men at the siege of Therougne, and
also at Tournai, and in the church at Tournai, on
September 25th, 1513, he was knighted by the King
under his banner, thus becoming a Knight Banneret.

He also had a special grant to himself and his heirs of an honourable augmentation out of the King's own royal ensign and devices, viz., a lion passant guardant, or, commonly spoken of as a lion of England, and for a crest a demidragon erased gules within a coronet of gold upon a torse argent, and vert. Also of a coat :—argent a chevron vert, within a bordure azure, besauté—green and white were Henry VIII.'s colours. It is a curious fact that the iron seal * of Thomas de Compton, found at Compton Wynyates, has a bearing of three fleur-de-lys and not the three esquires' helmets, to which Henry VIII. added for Sir William and his heirs the lion of England. Mr. Shirley of Eatington, in Warwick, an authority in such matters, was of opinion that the three helmets were described and figured in the grant of arms as those of the Comptons of Warwickshire by a blunder of the heralds of that day. They were undoubtedly the arms of the Comptons of Nottinghamshire, who may have been originally the same family.

To return to Sir William Compton. In 1513 he was made Chancellor of Ireland, with leave to perform the office by deputy. Afterwards he was

---

* This iron seal has round a shield the words 'Sr Thoma de Compton.' In the shield is a chevron with three fleur-de-lys, and this bearing is given in Dugdale's copy of the Balliol window as part of the arms of Sir W. Compton.

GREAT HALL.

.

made Keeper of the Privy Purse. In 1520 he obtained licence to impark land in Over Compton and Nether Compton, alias 'Compton Vyneyates,' in Warwickshire. In 1523 he took part in certain raids into Scotland, and the destruction of various fortresses. Cardinal Wolsey was the cause of his being sent there, 'who perceiving in what favour he grew with the King, contrived to pack him out of the way, lest in time he might diminish his greatness.'

A patent dated February 23rd, 1527, gave him licence to keep his hat on in the King's presence. He enjoyed the King's favour till his death of the sweating sickness in 1528, when the inventory of his goods valued his movables at 4485*l*., money owed to him at 1900*l*., and the debts he owed at 1000*l*. He directed by his will that an alabaster monument should be put up to the memory of his father and mother, and left an ivory chest with a gilt lock, and with jewels and treasures inside, to the King, together with 1000 marks. He left his 'wedding gown of tinsell sattin' to be made into a vestment. The executor had to pay 1000*l*. to be allowed to prove the will.

Sir William Compton left his estates to his son Peter. After Wolsey's death, he was ward to George Talbot, Earl of Shrewsbury, who married him before he was nineteen to his daughter Anne, heiress, through her mother, to Sir R. Walden. He died a minor and left an infant heir, Henry, born in 1542. He was described as 'a person of fine wit and solid judgment,' and was summoned to Parliament as Baron Compton in 1572. The following year he settled a great lawsuit, which he had for some time been carrying on with the Earl of Kent about the Northamptonshire property. For it seems that one Richard, Earl of Kent, a great waster and spend-thrift, who had sold Castle Ashby to Sir William Compton in 1512, had no right to sell it, the will which he produced for that purpose being a forgery. His brother, who had succeeded him, was too poor to prosecute his claims, and it was not till two generations later that his heir could afford to take the title of Earl of Kent, and seek his rights in a court of law. The suit never proceeded to judgment, but was compounded by Lord Compton ceding part of the property and paying 1400*l.* for the rest, thus in fact buying it a second time. The site of the old Castle of Ashby had been let on a long lease as a grazing ground; in 1583 the lease fell in, and Lord Compton began to build there soon after. His arms and those of his first wife, Frances Hastings, daughter of the Earl of Huntingdon, appear on the small door of the S.W. tower of Castle Ashby. He did not make any alterations in Compton Wynyates, unless he removed some of the wooden windows

FRONT DOOR FROM INTERIOR.

and put in stone mullions, which are very much alike to those of Castle Ashby. He was one of the Peers assigned for trial of the Queen of Scots, and died in 1589. The date of the birth of his son William is not recorded; but he is the hero of a romantic story, and by marrying the richest heiress of the day brought additional great wealth into the family.

It seems that he fell in love with Miss Spencer, daughter of a wealthy citizen of London, who was Lord Mayor in 36 Elizabeth, and who was proverbially known at the time as 'Rich Spencer.' Sir John Spencer by no means approved of the advances of the young courtier, and positively refused his consent to their marriage. On this Lord Compton bribed the baker to let him take in the loaves for the Mayoral household one early morning. As soon as the bread was out of the basket the lady stepped in, and Lord Compton was boldly carrying away his precious load when he was met by Sir John, who, luckily not recognising him, gave him a sixpence as a reward for being so early, telling him it was the way to thrive. On discovering, however, what had happened, he was so angry that he disinherited his daughter, and the quarrel was only made up by Queen Elizabeth, who invited the Lord Mayor to stand sponsor with her for a child in whom she was much interested. The unsuspicious grandfather went to

The Family History to the Civil War

Windsor, promised to adopt the child, who was
christened Spencer, and then the disinherited couple
were brought in and a complete reconciliation followed.
Good Queen Bess did a good turn that day for the
Compton family, for all Sir John's wealth was left
to Lord Compton, his son-in-law. On the death of
Sir John, in 1610, he left (according to the lowest
accounts) 300,000*l.*—a prodigious sum in those days.
Lord Compton was so overwhelmed with the news of
his succession to such wealth that he inconsequently
went out of his mind. He soon got better, but had a
relapse, which may have been caused by the following
letter written him by his wife. The former corre-
spondence to which it refers is lost:—

' My sweet life,

' Now I have declared to you my mind for the
settling of youre state. I suppose that it were best
for me to bethink or consider with myself what
allowance were meetest for me. For considering
what care I have had of your estate, and how respect-
fully I dealt with those which by the laws of God, of
nature, and of civil polity, wit, religion, government
and honesty, you my dear are bound to, I pray and
beseech you to grant me 600*l.* per annum quarterly
to be paid. Also I would (besides that allowance for
my apparel) have 600*l.* added yearly (quarterly to be

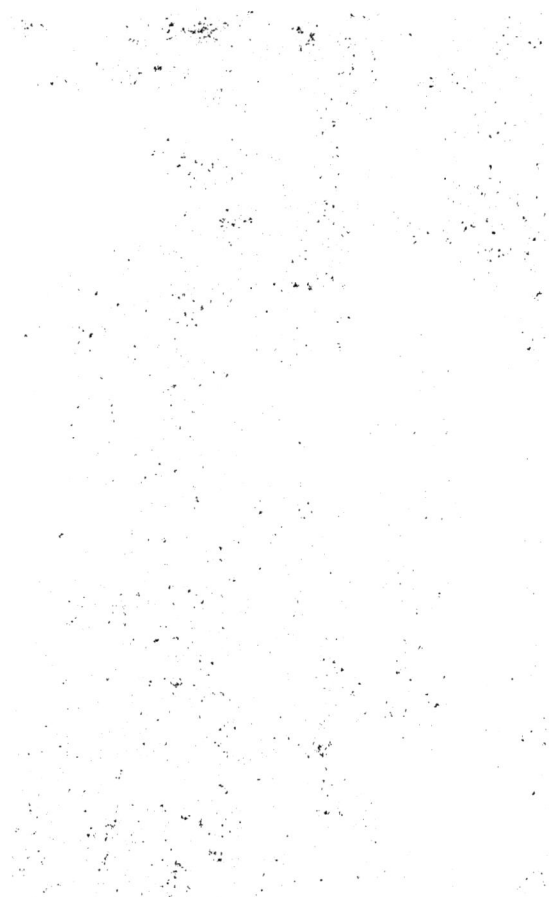

...be child, who was
...disinherited couple
...ciliation followed
...that day for the
...wealth was left
...the death of
...the lowest
...those days.
...news of
...quietly
...but had a
...following
...after corre-

...you may hold for the
...purpose that it were best
...myself what
...considering
...their respect-
...es of God, of
...government
...to, I pray and
...annum quarterly
...but allowance for
...quarterly to be

SUNDIAL IN THE BEST GARDEN.

paid) for the performance of charitable works; and those things I would not, neither will be accountable for. Also I will have three horses for my own saddle, that none shall dare to lend or borrow, none lend but I, none borrow but you. Also I would have two gentlewomen lest one should be sick or have some other let, also believe that it is an undecent thing for a gentlewoman to stand mumping alone, when God hath blessed their lord and lady with a good estate. Also when I ride a hunting or hawking, or travel from one house to another, I will have them attending, so for either of the said women I must and will have for either of them a horse. Also I will have six or eight gentlemen, and I will have my two coaches, one lined with velvet to myself with four very fair horses, and a coach for my women, lined with sweet cloth, one laced with gold, the other with scarlet and laced with watchet lace and silver with four good horses. Also I will have two coachmen, one for my own coach, the other for my women. Also at any time when I travel I will be allowed not only carroches and spare horses for me and my women, but I will have such carriages as shall be fitting for all orderly not pestering my things with my women's, nor theirs with chambermaids, nor theirs with washmaids. Also for laundresses when I travel I will have them sent away before the carriages to see all safe, and the chambermaids I will have go before with the greens (rushes) that the chambers may be ready, sweet and clean. Also for that it is undecent to crowd up myself with my gentleman usher in my coach, I will have him to have a convenient horse to attend me either in city or in country and I must have two footmen and my desire is that you defray all the charges for me. And for myself besides my yearly allowance I would have twenty gowns of apparel, six of them excellent good ones. Also I would have 6000*l.* to buy me jewels, and 4000*l.* to buy me a pearl chain.

'Now seeing I am so reasonable with you I pray you to find my children apparel and their schooling, and also my servants (men and women) their wages. Also I will have my houses furnished and all my lodging chambers to be suited with all such furniture as is fit, as beds, stools, chairs, suitable cushions, carpets, silver warming pans, cupboards of plate, fine hangings and such like; so for my drawing chambers in all houses I will have them delicately furnished, both with hangings, couch, canopy, glass, carpet, chair cushions, and all things thereunto belonging. Also my desire is that you pay all my debts, build Ashby House, and purchase lands, and lend no money (as you love God) to the Lord Chamberlain, who would have all, perhaps your life from you. You know him, God keep me and you from such as he is.

with the greens (riches?)
... ready, sweet and cl...
... crown up myself with
... b I will have him to
... me either in city
... two footmen and say
... ges for me. And
... since I would have
... at excellent good
... to buy me jewels, and

... able with you I pray
... and their schooling,
... and ... their wages,
... furnished and all my
... be stored with all such furnitures
... as beds, stools, chairs, suitable cushions
... silver ... pans, cupboards of plate ...
... and ... so ... my drawing chambers
... hence ... delicately furnished,
... nopy, glass, carpet, chair
... belonging. Also
... all ... dolls, but I Ashby
... lands, and I nd no money as
... the Lord Chamberlain, who would
... your life to you. You know him,
... and you ... such as he is.

MOAT GARDEN.

'So now I have declared to you what I would have, and what that is that I would not have, I pray that when you be an Earl to allow me 1000*l.* more than I now desire, and double attendance.

The Family History to the Civil War

'Your loving wife,

'ELIZA COMPTON.'

There is no date to this letter, but it evidently was written after Lord Compton succeeded to his father-in-law's property, and after Sir John's death in 1610. The lady had been brought up with a clear idea how to spend the fortune she brought into the family, even supposing it to have amounted, as some then supposed, to 800,000*l.* She makes no reference to Compton Wynyates, which perhaps was not grand enough for her extravagant taste, but desires that Ashby House be built. This must have meant, as in the case of Sir William Compton, and Compton Wynyates, alterations and embellishments. Inigo Jones made designs for the purpose, in which he proposed to alter all that Lord Northampton's father had erected. His plans were only partially carried out, but the lady's notions of building (which must have been pretty large to provide accommodation for her gentlemen, gentle-women, chambermaids and laundrymaids, coachmen and footmen) happily found a safe outlet at Castle Ashby, without destroying the old Warwickshire

manor-house of Henry VIII.'s time. Inigo Jones
seems, however, to have put ceilings to one or two of
the Compton Wynyates rooms, as some of them are
very like those at Castle Ashby, one of them having
the arms of Compton and of Spencer on separate
shields. These ceilings at Compton Wynyates are in
the dining-room on the ground floor, and in the drawing-room which looks into the chapel. In the bedroom called Henry VIII.'s. room is a ceiling with the
arms of Henry VIII., Elizabeth, James I. and
Charles I. This therefore must have been put here
by the next Lord Northampton, as may be also that in
the guard-room, which corresponds closely to one in
a room at Castle Ashby, in which the walls were de-
corated by Spencer, Lord Northampton and his wife,
their arms appearing over the fireplace and in the
border of the panelling.

William, Lord Compton, died in 1630. He had
been made K.C.B. by Elizabeth, and in 15 James I.
was appointed Lieutenant within the principality of
Wales. The next year he was created Earl of Northampton, and was given the Garter. His last illness
was caused by an imprudence which throws an odd
light on the customs of the day. This is the story:
' Yesterday sen'night the Earl of Northampton, Lord
President of Wales (after he had waited on the King
at supper and had also supped), went in a boat with

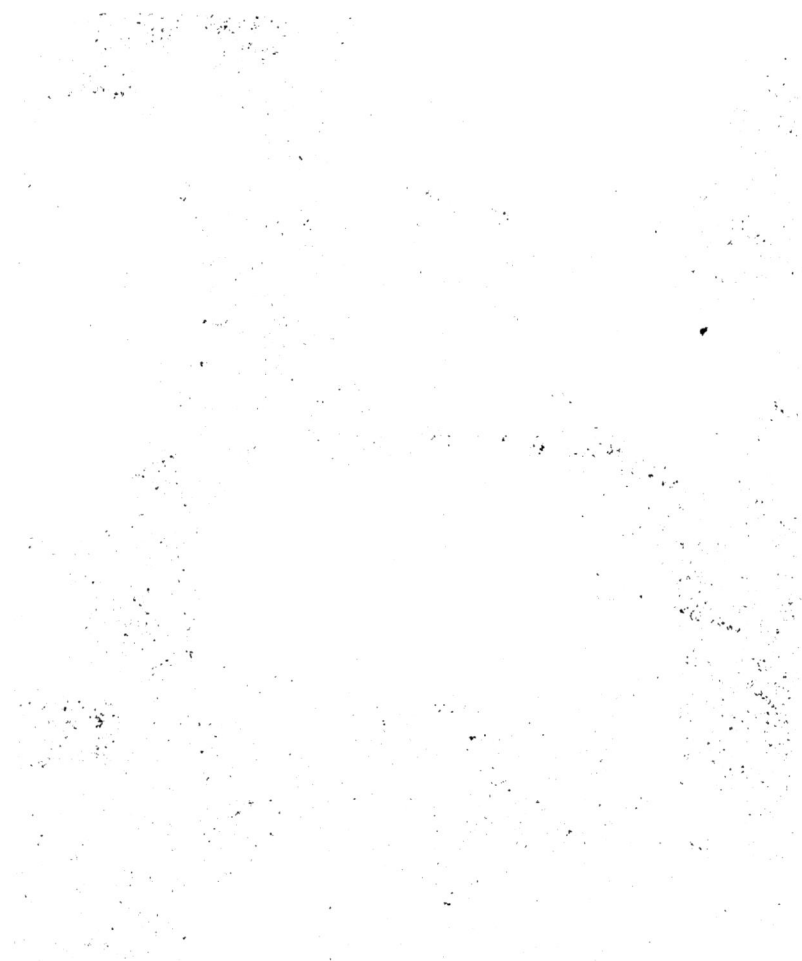

COMPTON WYNYATES

Henry VIII's time, Inigo Jones ... ... belongs to one or two of ... ... as some of them are ... ... one of them having ... of Spencer on separate ... ... Compton Wynyates are in ... ... and in the draw- ... ... ped. In the bed- ... ... ending with the Henry ... VIII, Elizabeth, James I and ... ... have been put here ... ... as may be a'so that in ... ... closely to one ... ... the walls were ... ... Compton and his wi ... ... over the fireplace and in t! ... of the panels.

Wil ... Lord ... ... died in 1630. He ... ... Elizabeth, and in 15 James I ... in the principality of ... created Earl of No ... ... His last ... ... which throws ... ... This is the story: ... Northampton. Lord ... ... on the hill ... ... upon ... in a hot wa ...

DOVECOT   .

others to wash himself in the Thames, and so soon as *The Family* *History to* his legs were in the water but to the knees he had the *the Civil* *War* colic, and cried out, "Have me into the boat again, for I am a dead man," and died a few hours after, at his lodgings in the Savoy.'

CHAPTER V.

HISTORY OF THE COMPTON FAMILY DURING AND
AFTER THE CIVIL WAR.

The Family History after the Civil War
HE was succeeded by Spencer, who took his part in the Civil War, when the family place was to experience some changes owing to that disturbed period. It is recorded that Spencer in his youth 'discovered so great a genius that it was as much as four several tutors at home, at Cambridge, in France, and in Italy, each taking his respective hour for the art and science he professed, could keep pace with his great proficiency.' He was a favourite of Charles I. when Prince of Wales, and accompanied him to Spain in 1622. He assisted at his coronation as Master of the Robes, and though a 'Staffordian' he was loyal to the King and a defender of the 'true Protestant religion.' When the Civil War broke out he was reported as the best furnished with arms of any nobleman in the kingdom. He commanded 2000 men at the battle of Edgehill, a few miles from Compton Wynyates; he took Banbury, which was held by his son to the end of the Civil War, and was afterwards killed at Hopton Heath. In that battle, just as it was

88

COMPTON CREST IN BAY WINDOW.

won, his horse was killed under him: he was sur- rounded by the enemy and offered quarter. This he refused, answering that 'he scorned to take quarter from such base rogues and rebels as they were.' He died fighting to the last. His eldest son James asked for the body, but it was refused unless all the fruits of victory were relinquished, and he was buried in Derby by the Parliamentarians.

His six sons were all distinguished Royalists. The three eldest fought under their father, and the fourth, who was still too young to grasp a pistol, cried with indignation that he was not allowed to expose himself to the same hazard as his brothers.

Spencer was succeeded by his eldest son James, who had been at the battle of Edgehill and was wounded at Hopton Heath, but a few weeks later was fighting again with Prince Rupert at Lichfield. In June, 1644, Colonel Purefoy, a Parliamentarian, reached Compton Wynyates with 400 foot and 300 horse; these lay before it for two days, drove the park and killed the deer, defaced the monuments in the church, and ultimately took the house, and 14 officers and 120 soldiers prisoners. He also seized 5000*l.* in money, 80 horses, 400 sheep, 160 head of cattle, and 18 loads of plunder, besides 6 earthen pots of money found in the fish-pond.

There is a family tradition that a considerable

number of Cavaliers who had been wounded in the attack remained in the house when it was taken, that they were concealed in the roofs by Lady Northampton, who subsequently, in a petition to Parliament, stated that she had 'neither contributed or intermeddled with or in this unhappy war.' The roofs at that time were entered by a trap-door, and the Royalist soldiers were there tended by her, and finally left the house without the Puritan garrison knowing anything about it.

The latter continued to hold the house till the surrender of Banbury in 1646, but during that period had to sustain a violent attack from the Comptons and part of the garrison of Banbury. The account as written by the Governor, Sergeant Purefoy, to his Colonel throws some light on the defensive arrangements of the house at that time.

After a few expressions of pious thankfulness, he reports :—

'This night about 2 of ye clock about 1000 or 1200 horse and foot' (there were in fact about 300) 'of ye enemies fell upon me at Compton, stormed my outworks, gained my stables, and cut down my great drawbridge, possessed themselves of all my troop of horses, and took about 30 of my foot-soldiers in their beds, who lay over ye stables, and all this was done almost before a man could think what to do. We

STONE HEAD IN COURTYARD LEADING FROM BUTTERY HATCH.

received this fierce alarm as we had good cause and presently made good ye new sconce before ye stone bridge, and beat them out of ye great court, there being about 200 men entered, and ready to storm ye sconce. But we gave them so hot a sally that we forced them to retreat back to ye stables, barns and brewhouse, where from ye windows they played very hot upon us. I then commanded Lieutenant Purefoy and my Quartermaster, having no other officers of quality at home, ye rest being abroad with about 300 of my best troopers, to sally upon ye enemy with a party of some 40, and so attempt the regaining of the brewhouse and ye rooms above, which instantly they did with ye most gallant resolution and courage. This party I say, fought thus with the enemy and came to push of pike, nay to ye sword's point, and laid about them so bravely that they forced the enemy to fly before them from chamber to chamber, whereupon I presently sent my younger brother ye Ensign with three corporals of horse, and about 40 men more to relieve ye first party, and I assure you, Sir, ye boy fought well, and led on his men most bravely, and relieved his brother by which means all the upper rooms were regained. And now ye enemy kept only ye stables and ye barns which they held stoutly, but my resolute soldiers did so thunder their horse and reserves of foot that stood within pistol shot, that Sir William and Sir Charles Compton, who were there present began to give ground, which my soldiers easily perceiving, some leapt out at ye windows, and so into ye outworks, by which means I recovered my outworks again, and made a sally port by which ye enemy endeavoured to retreat at, but finding they were frustrated of their hopes, and that my musketeers did play so hot upon ye great drawbridge, that they could not be relieved, and withal we, having beaten ye enemy out of their work which we stormed when you took ye house, I had time thereby to recover fully ye great drawbridge, and instantly got new ropes and new locks and drew it up again in spite of them all. Now by this means all those whose names are herewith enclosed to you are in Cobs pound, having no means in ye world to retreat. Whereupon they fought desperately for ye space of three hours and ye valiant Comptons perceiving their extreme loss, attempted three several times to storm and regain my outworks, but all ye three times were beaten off with as much resolution and gallantry of my soldiers as could be expressed by men. Ye enemy within set fire to all ye hay, straw, and all ye combustible stuff to smother my men out of ye upper rooms, which did indeed much annoy them, and ye enemy without threw at least an hundred hand grenades on ye houses, so as they set them on fire in three several places, where-

STEPS FROM THE LAWN INTO 'BEST GARDEN.

upon Sir Charles and Sir William thinking all then
over sent a trumpeter to parley, but I commanded
that none should parley nor would I permit ye trumpeter to speak at all unto me, and fain would he have
said something to my soldiers, but I commanded him
upon his life to be gone and not return any more upon
his peril, and we continued to fight still, and ye
aforesaid fire did so increase that I thought it fit to
offer quarter to them that were in ye stable for their
lives only, but they would not hear me. Upon which
I drew all my men together and fell violently upon
them, in which assault were slain and taken prisoners
all whose names are in ye ensuing list. This did so
dishearten ye Comptons and all their forces that they
presently drew off all their foot and only faced me
with their horse.

'And thus we were clearly rid of them. Sir, this
is as true and short a narrative as I can conveniently
give you.

'I am, as we all are,

'Your obliged servants and kinsmen,

'GEORGE AND WILLIAM PUREFOY.

'Compton, Jan. 30th 1644' (*i.e.* '45).

'We recovered all our men again that ye enemy
had taken.

'A list of ye officers and soldiers slain and taken
43

prisoners: Captains 3, Lieutenants 2, one Ensign, one Quartermaster, one Cornet, 5 Corporals, 3 Sergeants, troopers and foot soldiers about 50; besides 6 cartloads of wounded men carried off, and near upon 40 common soldiers left dead behind them in and about ye garrison. Of mine own men both horse and foot only one man was desperately wounded, and another was slightly hurt, but no one I say was slain: a rare and wonderful providence indeed. We took of ye enemies horse and foot arms, &c., 150 muskets, 40 pistols and about 20 hand grenades.'

Another letter from Major Bridges gives the same account with the names of some of the officers killed or wounded, but the following account appeared in the Court periodical:—

'Saturday, Feb. 1st. The rebels tell us they have taken above 100 officers and soldiers from the garrison of Banbury: indeed on Tuesday last his Majesties forces from Banbury went within the outworks of Compton House and took 44 horse out of the stables, most of which the Rebels regained with a few Banbury men surprized in their quarters coming home from Compton: but for those officers whom the Rebels mention in print, they having taken a Banbury Quartermaster with his rolle, were thereby enabled to take so many names prisoners, the men themselves being safe in Banbury.'

SOUTH EAST VIEW OF HOUSE.

COMPTON WYNYATES

Whatever may have been the number slain or taken prisoners, the attempt of the Comptons to retake their house failed, and the Parliamentarians' account, if exaggerated, is useful in its details of the outworks of the house. It proves that besides the moat which surrounded the house, there was a second moat in front of a great court with a drawbridge; that outside the two moats there were outworks, and in the court were stables, brewhouse and barns; that a stone bridge crossed the inner moat and a sconce guarded it. The Royal forces having surprised some of the outworks cut down the great drawbridge and thus admitted them into the court where they seized the stables and prepared to storm the sconce. The garrison making a sally across the bridge drove some of them out beyond the drawbridge, others taking refuge in the barns, brewhouse, and stables. The garrison thus cleared the brewhouse, regained the outworks, and with new ropes and locks drew up the drawbridge, entrapping the men in the stables. The Compton forces being thus divided, those without made several unsuccessful attacks on the outworks, while those within tried to smoke out the garrison by setting fire to the barns. They were however killed or taken prisoners, and the Comptons with their men outside withdrew to Banbury.

The garrison at Compton do not appear to have

*The Family
History
after the
Civil War* been very comfortable, for the Court newspaper stated that Major Purefoy was so cooped up by the Earl of Northampton, 'that his comings abroad are more like a thief than a souldier, creeping sometimes in the darke where he steales contributions to keep himselfe in heart to pen blustering warrants.' Lord Northampton with his brother was especially active between Northampton and Banbury, and they were very successful, except in their attacks on Compton. Can it have been that they fought more gently when they were dealing with the house they loved, and that the fear of damaging their home weakened their attack? The brothers fought well together, for in an account of an encounter with the enemy's cavalry near Northampton, Lord Northampton had his head-piece beaten off; Sir Charles Compton escaped death only by the pistol of his adversary missing fire; Sir William Compton's horse was shot under him; and Sir Spencer Compton was at one time surrounded by eight adversaries. All the four, however, escaped without personal hurt; though it is said they ' charged and rescued one another so often, that if any of the foure had been absent some one of them might have fallen.'

In 1644 Banbury Castle had been successfully defended and held by Sir William, then twenty-one years old, whom Cromwell called the 'sober young man.

HOUSE FROM THE PERGOLA.

and godly cavalier.' Though the garrison was reduced by siege to such straits that 'they had but two horses uneaten,' they held out until relieved by Lord Northampton. Lord William had not slept in bed for thirteen weeks! The castle and town of Banbury must have required constant restoration, as the following order shows, which was found in 1844 among some rubbish when a cottage was taken down in Bodicote, near Banbury.

'To the constables of Bandicott :—

'Thes are in his Maj^ts name streightely to chardge to commande you That you bring before me to the Castle of Banburye tomorrow morninge by the seaven of the clocke All the masons, carpenters and sawyers wth your Towneshipp and all their working Tooles ther to be ymploied in his Maj^ts service. Hereof faile you nott uppō paine of Death dated at Banburye Castle the 9th of Februarye 1645.

'W. COMPTON.'

In January 1646 it was again besieged, and after a protracted and gallant defence was surrendered next year on honourable terms when the King had fled to Scotland. On June 16th the Parliamentary troops were withdrawn from Compton Wynyates and the outworks were destroyed.

To this year Dugdale, in his History of Warwickshire, refers the destruction of the Church, but it must

47

have occurred two years before, namely in 1644, when the Cromwellians seized the house. Dugdale writes: 'As for the fabric thereof, it is now totally reduced to rubbish, having been demolished when Compton House was garrisoned by the Parliament forces, the monuments therein to Sir William Compton and his Lady (temp: Henry VIII.) with that of Henry Lord Compton, his grandson (1527–1589) which were very beautiful and stately being utterly razed and knocked to pieces.' The story runs that the destruction of the church was accidental, though it cannot be supposed that the Cromwellians were sorry to do mischief to the Comptons' church. Their cannon is said to have been placed on the opposite hill to destroy the house, but owing to the great depth at which it lies, the balls, passing over it, battered and destroyed the church beyond. Fragments of the monuments can be seen in the present church, having been found in the moat, where they could hardly have been thrown by accident. They are recumbent marble figures of two men and three women, evidently the monuments of Sir William Compton and his wife, and their grandson Henry with his two wives. The latter in his will ordered 'his body to be buried at Compton in such sort as should be seemly to his calling, and that a tomb should be made for him with his picture and both his wives.' The church was rebuilt at the Restoration.

48

... lately in 164? when
... house. Dugdale writes:
... is now totally reduced to
... described when Compton
... the Parliament forces, the
... William Compton and his
... with that of Henry Lord
... 1622-1689, which were very
... only razed and knocked
... that the destruction of the
... church it cannot be supposed
... were very to do mischief to
... Their cannon is said to have
... hill to destroy the house,
... that which it lies, the balls,
... and destroyed the church
... of the monuments can be seen
... having been found in the most,
... hardly have been thrown by
... recumbent marble figures of two
... evidently the monuments of
... and his wife, and their grand-
... two wives. The latter in his will
... only to be buried at Compton in such sort
... only to his calling, and that a tomb
... be made for him with his picture and both his
... The church was rebuilt at the Restoration.

48

PERGOLA IN 'BEST GARDEN'.

COMPTON WYNYATES

James, Lord Northampton, was continually fight- ing until the King's cause was completely lost, when he was ordered with other officers to go beyond the seas. He avoided, however, expatriation by taking the necessary oaths, and having paid 15,000*l.*, after many petitions, compounded his estates in 1650. In one petition he stated that: 'being in his minority he was not only induced by the example but necessitated by the command of his late father (upon whose dispensation his support wholly depended) to engage in the late difference between the King and Parliament in which his father had lost his life, leaving a debt of above 30,000*l.* to be paid, and seven younger children to be provided for out of his estate which had been grievously wasted by the misfortunes of the times.'

He lived in retirement until the Restoration, when he attended the entry of Charles II. into London with a troop of 200 gentlemen clothed in blue and grey. He occupied several high positions until his death in 1681. He was buried at Compton Wynyates, having rebuilt the church.

A few words as to his mother and brothers may be of interest. His mother appears to have remained at Compton after it was taken by the enemy for a year at least, as there is a letter from Sir William Compton at Banbury, asking the Parliamentary General to give his mother a safe-conduct with her retinue to that

H

town. The General sent a very civil answer that at
the Council of War the next day: 'I shall propounde
your desires and second them with the best agreement I can.' He, however, wrote to his superiors that
he was convinced the trumpeter with the letter was
sent as a spy, and later on informed Sir William that
he had not yet received any answer from London.
Lady Northampton must somehow have moved to
Oxford, for in her petition to the 'Committee com-
pounding for delinquent estates,' she states that in
the beginning of these sad distractions she lived not
far distant from Oxford, 'and the outrage of the
souldiers in those parts grew so high that your
petitioner being a woman and destitute of former
friends with four small children conceived herself not
to be safe, &c. Whereupon she was necessitated to
make her abode in Oxford.' She probably was allowed
to compound for her estates, which were her jointure,
and retired to Grendon, near Castle Ashby, for the
remainder of her life.

Sir Charles Compton, the second son, who distinguished himself, though only nineteen, at the battle
of Edgehill, and afterwards at Hopton Heath and
many other actions, was in great favour with
Charles II., but was killed by a fall from his horse at
Northampton at the early age of thirty-eight.

Sir William Compton, the third son, was eighteen

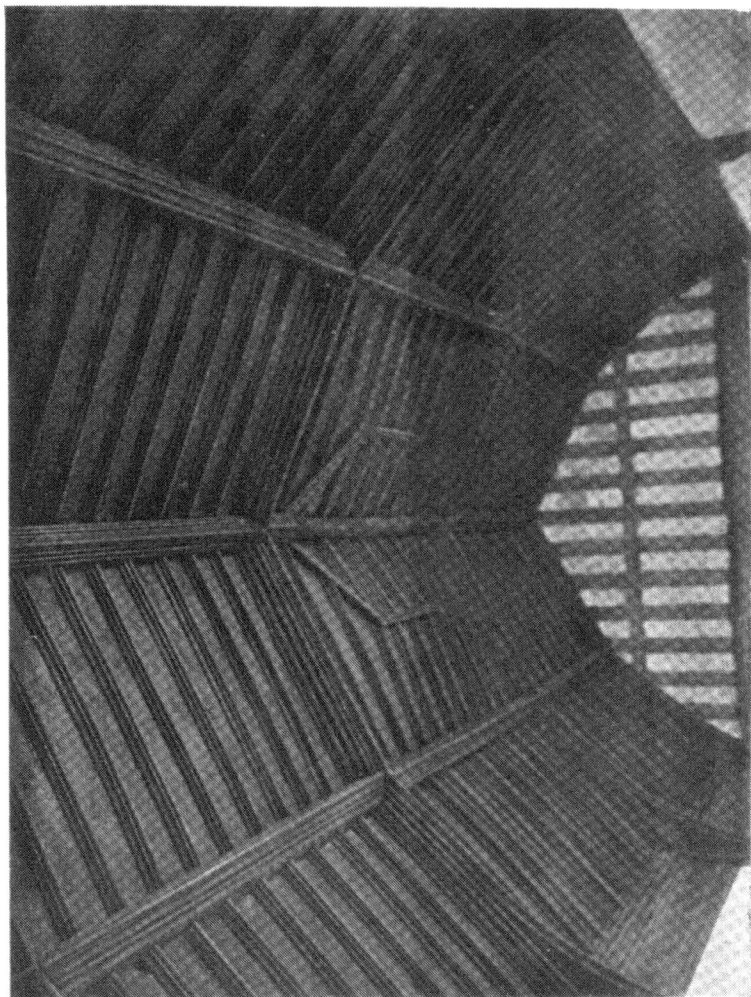

ROOF OF GREAT HALL

when the Civil War broke out, and was Major-General *The Family History after the Civil War* of the Royal forces at Colchester at the age of twenty-four. At the Restoration he was made a Privy Councillor and Major-General of His Majesty's Ordnance. He died at the age of thirty-nine.

Sir Spencer Compton was only thirteen when he was not allowed to take part in the Battle of Edgehill, but a year or two later he is found fighting with his brothers. He had a deeply religious character: ' a discreet piety towards the first Being, a sober and due government of his own actions, and a public justice and kindness towards all men; confining all thoughts of glory within the compass of virtue, thinking nothing more dishonourable than sin. If he had a fault it was that he rather chose to hide, than to exercise his virtue.' He followed Charles II. into exile and died at Bruges in 1659, at the age of thirty, his dying words to his two friends, Bishop Morley and Dr. Erles, being: ' O be good and keep close to the Principle of the Christian Religion, for this will bring a man peace at the last.'

Sir Francis Compton must have been a twin-brother of Sir Spencer. He was also a soldier, who, after the Restoration, rose to be Lieutenant-General of the Horse, and Lieutenant-Colonel of the regiment of Horse Guards. He was M.P. for Warwickshire from 1661 to 1679. He died in 1716, aged eighty-seven, the oldest Field Officer in Great Britain, 'having acquitted himself with honour and fidelity,' and was buried in Fulham churchyard, near his brother, the Bishop.

Henry Compton, sixth and youngest son, was only ten at the time of the Battle of Edgehill, and only entered the Army after the Restoration. He was a linguist and a scholar, and was persuaded by his friends to go into the Church. He therefore went to Cambridge, and afterwards to Oxford, and took his degree at both Colleges, and at the age of thirty-seven took his degree of Doctor of Divinity. He was elected Bishop of Oxford in 1674, and Bishop of London in 1765, and continued in good repute until James II. became King, whose measures he opposed and was in consequence suspended. He was called the Protestant Bishop, as he sturdily opposed anything approaching to Popery, and, espousing the Orange cause, took the place of the Archbishop of Canterbury at the Coronation of William and Mary. By his votes in the House of Lords he appears to have been very independent, and was not always in agreement with William III. When, however, Queen Anne succeeded, he 'rode in jackboots' in the procession of her entry into London, and was the chief adviser of the Queen. He was a botanist, for we owe to him the introduction of many of our trees and plants from abroad. He died at the age of eighty-one, and was buried in Fulham churchyard, where his monument has this inscription:

'H. LONDON

MDCCXIII.'

The Greek words are part of the words of St. Paul, Galatians, vi. 14, ' God forbid that I should glory *save in the cross* of Jesus Christ.' This ends the story of the six brothers, who, during the troublous times of the Stuarts and afterwards, played no inconspicuous part.

James, Lord Northampton, was succeeded, 1681, by his son George, who lived chiefly at Compton Wynyates, for by entries in an old household book of 1722, he paid a visit to London and then returned to Warwickshire, of which county he was Lord-Lieutenant. He was deprived of this position for opposing James II., as his uncle, the Bishop, was also deprived of his bishopric. He seems to have followed the lead of his uncle, as he recovered his honours at the accession of William and Mary, and carried the King's sceptre with the cross at their Coronation. He received King William at Castle Ashby; and continued to flourish under Queen Anne and George I., until his death in 1727. He made alterations in the drawing-rooms at Compton, and it is thought that he removed the mullions of the windows and put in sashes, which were ultimately replaced by mullions in 1860. In one of the rooms, now called the Cavalier's room, slips of paper were found in 1860, pasted on the walls, showing the heights of George's children and grandchildren. These unfortunately disappeared during reparation. He was succeeded by James, fifth Earl, who was called to the House of Lords as Baron Compton in 1711, and at the Coronation of George I. bore the ivory rod with the dove. He inherited from his uncle, Sir Spencer Compton, the estate of Wilmington in Sussex, who was Speaker of the House of Commons, and afterwards Prime Minister for a very short time. He was created Baron Wilmington, but, dying unmarried, the title went to his nephew, James. He was succeeded by his brother George, who was a member of Parliament, first for Tamworth, and then for many years for Northampton, until he became a Peer. Dying without issue, he was succeeded by his nephew, Charles, whose father was Consul-General in Portugal, and afterwards Envoy Extraordinary at the Court of Portugal. Charles, like his father, became Ambassador, and was appointed to Venice, into which town he made a public entry with great magnificence, but his young wife died there the same month, and the Ambassador died at Lyons on his way home a few months afterwards. There is a family legend that they were both *The Family History after the Civil War* poisoned by an Italian, but as a matter of fact they died of consumption. Their only daughter, Lady Betty, married into the Cavendish family and took with her the Compton plate, pictures, jewellery, and lace.

The Ambassador's brother, Spencer, succeeded him, and the account of the ruin of the family in his time has already been given.

The fortunes of the family were restored by his son Charles' marriage with a Miss Smith, an heiress, but the old house was left unfurnished and empty. It is only of late years that the Comptons have once more lived at Compton Wynyates, and with great and reverent care have put the house in order, have planted creepers on its walls, have restored the old garden, and with thankfulness for its preservation enjoy once more the loveliness of a perfect English Home.

Milton Keynes UK
Ingram Content Group UK Ltd.
UKHW022024110923
428497UK00005B/117

9 781016 085410